THE
MARTIN LUTHER KING, JR.,
COMPANION

THE
MARTIN LUTHER KING, JR.,
COMPANION

QUOTATIONS
FROM THE SPEECHES,
ESSAYS, AND BOOKS OF
MARTIN LUTHER KING, JR.

SELECTED BY
CORETTA SCOTT KING

INTRODUCTION BY
DEXTER SCOTT KING

ST. MARTIN'S PRESS   NEW YORK

Grateful acknowledgment is made for permission to reprint from the following:

Stride Toward Freedom by Martin Luther King, Jr. Copyright © 1957 by Martin Luther King, Jr.; copyright © renewed 1988 by Coretta Scott King, Dexter Scott King, Martin Luther King III, Yolanda King, and Bernice King. Reprinted by permission of HarperCollins Publishers Inc.

Why We Can't Wait by Martin Luther King, Jr. Copyright © 1963, 1964 by Martin Luther King, Jr. Copyright © renewed 1991 by Coretta Scott King. Reprinted by permission of HarperCollins Publishers Inc.

Where Do We Go from Here: Chaos or Community? by Martin Luther King, Jr. Copyright © 1967 by Martin Luther King, Jr. Reprinted by permission of HarperCollins Publishers Inc.

The Trumpet of Conscience by Martin Luther King, Jr. Copyright © 1967 by Martin Luther King, Jr. Reprinted by permission of HarperCollins Publishers Inc.

Design by Dawn Niles

ISBN 0-312-09063-3

First Edition: February 1993

10   9   8   7   6   5   4   3   2   1   0

I am convinced that the universe is under the control of a loving purpose, and that in the struggle for righteousness man has cosmic companionship. Behind the harsh appearance of the world there is a benign power.

—Martin Luther King, Jr.

My gratitude to Joe H. Kirchberger for his knowledgeable assistance on this selection of *The Martin Luther King, Jr., Companion*.

—Coretta Scott King

CONTENTS

PART FOUR: PHILOSOPHIES

PART FIVE: ISSUES

PART SIX: REFLECTIONS

SOURCES

Each quotation used in this volume is attributed directly to a particular book or speech by Martin Luther King, Jr. In the interest of space, only the source's initials are used in the text. The full titles are listed here.

STF   *Stride Toward Freedom: The Montgomery Story*
                New York: Harper, 1958

STL   *Strength to Love*
                New York: Harper, 1963

WCW   *Why We Can't Wait*
                New York: Harper, 1963

WDWG   *Where Do We Go from Here: Chaos or Community?*
                New York: Harper, 1967

TOC   *The Trumpet of Conscience*
                New York: Harper, 1968

NL   "Nobel Prize Lecture"
                December 11, 1968

VL   "Beyond Vietnam"
                Lecture, April 4, 1968

To most young people history is just that, with no relevance to the present or future. With our new technologies and new-found freedoms, what can we learn from a civil rights movement that took place before this generation was born? If we cannot understand and respect the lessons which our ancestors learned through hard struggle, then we are condemned to relive those same struggles over and over again. If history has taught us nothing else, it has taught us that.

Such lessons of history seem lost on so many people today, for the innocence of yesteryear, an innocence accompanied by righteous struggle, inequality, and deprivation, has, all too often, been replaced with a deep-seated indifference that nothing can change and nothing ever will. I maintain that this is not so. I know from my own childhood, from listening to the words of my father, just how vital a knowledge of one's heritage is. I also know just how vital every struggle is, and that each mountaintop can be scaled in time.

The Martin Luther King, Jr., Companion is a book about my father's words, but more significantly, it's a blueprint for social change. I feel that this portable companion can be read wholly on its own, but also as a source book that illuminates the passages of Dr. King's greatest works. This is a book that is just as meaningful, perhaps more relevant today, than it was twenty-five years ago, when my father died.

The Martin Luther King, Jr., Companion is the philosophy of a man whose love and brilliance brought the wisdom of the pulpit into a new realm, creating a message that will, I believe, transcend the ages. Divided into six sections, the book deals with thirty-two separate subjects, ranging from slavery to nonviolence, from the meaning of love and evil to the significance of Black Power. Along the way, I think you will feel as if you were almost reading a biography of Dr. King, for we follow him from Montgomery, where Rosa Parks dared to say no to a white man on a bus, to Birmingham, where the Klan blew up a church with four little girls inside, to the "I Have a Dream" speech, delivered in Washington, D.C., thirty years ago this year, and on to his fateful message in Memphis.

Above all, *The Martin Luther King, Jr., Companion* is a book about a calling; for my father's gifts of writing and oratory, developed early in his life, were so profound that they were indeed God-given. When you are in an environment where people, like my father's parents, were very spiritual, you get drawn by a higher power at work—most often with no control over the forces at hand. Once my father understood his calling, he had no problem surrendering himself to that will of God with an unfailing commitment to stay the path, no matter what the obstacles.

A lot of people today would have taken the easy way out, but my father tried to live a committed life. I often equate the kind of work he did with waging a war—that my father had enlisted in the service and that his life was one extended tour of duty.

It's hard to believe that with all my father's other duties and obligations, including his prolific writings (he wrote over 200,000 documents in his lifetime), he was also a devoted husband and father of four children. I was quite young at the time, but I remember him as being a very committed, compassionate father. When he would come home from long trips, he was extremely loving and playful, and he would relate to kids by telling jokes and displaying great humor. Although we did not have a large quantity of time to spend together, the quality of the time I spent with my father was both loving and memorable.

Love, coupled with truth, was what my father's life was all about. He believed that "truth crushed to earth would rise again." It seems today that so many kids concentrate solely on the ceremony of life, but not on its sacrament. Young people should read this book because it provides timeless inspiration. Dr. King's words contain many metaphors for life. His words of wisdom can be applied to any situation, any day. This is why, in contrast to so many other figures from the 1950s and 1960s, it is fair to state that the understanding of my father's legacy has grown. His is still so well received.

My father died at age thirty-nine, but he lived a life fuller than most who have found longevity. God's divine hand works in mysterious ways, and God sometimes removes those most holy for His own purpose. My father died for the glory of God and his death was a triumph because he always stayed with his mission.

Dexter Scott King
Atlanta, Georgia
January 1993

THE
MARTIN LUTHER KING, JR.,
COMPANION

PART ONE
HERITAGE

SLAVERY AND EMANCIPATION

Who are we? We are the descendants of slaves . . . we are the heirs of a past of rope, fire, and murder. I for one am not ashamed of this past. My shame is for those who became so inhuman that they could inflict this torture upon us.

—*WDWG* II

Since the institution of slavery was so important to the economic development of America, it had a profound impact in shaping the social-political-legal structure of the nation. Land and slaves were the chief forms of private property. In the service of this system, human beings were reduced to propertyless property.

—*WDWG* III

No one doubts the valor and commitment that characterized George Washington's life. But to the end of his days he maintained a posture of exclusionism toward the slave. He was a fourth-generation slaveholder. He only allowed Negroes to enter the Continental Army because His Majesty's Crown was attempting to recruit Negroes to the British cause.

—*WDWG* III

Many poor whites . . . were the derivative victims of slavery. As long as labor was cheapened by the involuntary servitude of the black man, the freedom of white labor, especially in the South, was little more than a myth.

—*WCW* VIII

It is because the Negro knows that no person—as well as no nation—can truly exist half slave and half free that he has embroidered upon his banners the significant word NOW.

—*WCW* VIII

Abraham Lincoln did not ask, "What will happen to me if I issue the Emancipation Proclamation and bring an end to chattel slavery?" but he asked, "What will happen to the Union and to millions of Negro people, if I fail to do it?"

—*STL* III

The Emancipation Proclamation [of 1863] did not, however, bring full freedom to the Negro, for although he enjoyed certain political and social opportunities during the Reconstruction, the Negro soon discovered that the pharaohs of the South were determined to keep him in slavery.

—*STL* VIII

Four million newly liberated slaves found themselves with no bread to eat, no land to cultivate, no shelter to cover their heads. . . . In 1863 the Negro was given abstract freedom expressed in luminous rhetoric. But in an agrarian economy he was given no land to make liberation concrete.

—*WDWG* III

BLACKS AND WHITES

Abused and scorned though we [the blacks] may be, our destiny is tied up with America's destiny. Before the Pilgrims landed at Plymouth, we were here. Before the pen of Jefferson etched the majestic words of the Declaration of Independence across the pages of history, we were here.

> —*WCW* V
> "Letter from Birmingham Jail"

Arnold Toynbee says in *A Study of History* that it may be the Negro who will give the new spiritual dynamic to Western civilization that it so desperately needs to survive. I hope this is possible. The spiritual power that the Negro can radiate to the world comes from love, understanding, good will, and nonviolence.

> —*STF* XI

Many white men fear retaliation. The job of the Negro is to show them that they have nothing to fear, that the Negro understands and forgives and is ready to forget the past.

> —*STF* XI

There are those who are sufficiently soft-minded to believe in the superiority of the white race and the inferiority of the Negro in spite of the tough-minded research of anthropologists who reveal the falsity of such a notion.

> —*STL* I

Even semantics have conspired to make that which is black seem ugly and degrading. In *Roget's Thesaurus* there are some 120 synonyms for "blackness," and at least 60 of them are offensive—such words as "blot," "soot," "crime," "devil," and "foul." There are some 134 synonyms for "whiteness," and all are favorable. . . .

—WDWG II

It was argued that the Negro was inferior by nature because of Noah's curse upon the children of Ham. . . . The greatest blasphemy of the whole ugly process was that the white man ended up making God his partner in the exploitation of the Negro.

—WDWG III

In the final analysis the white man cannot ignore the Negro's problem, because he is part of the Negro and the Negro is part of him. The Negro's agony diminishes the white man, and the Negro's salvation enlarges the white man.

—WDWG III

Young Negroes had traditionally imitated whites in dress, conduct, and thought in a rigid, middle-class pattern. . . . Now they ceased imitating and began initiating. Leadership passed into the hands of Negroes, and their white allies began learning from them.

—TOC III

THE AFRICAN-AMERICAN MENTALITY

. . . when your first name becomes "nigger," your middle name becomes "boy" (however old you are), and your wife and mother are never given the respected title "Mrs."; when you are harried by day and haunted by night by the fact that you are a Negro . . . when you are forever fighting a degenerating sense of "nobodiness"—then you will understand why we find it difficult to wait.

—*WCW* V
"Letter from Birmingham Jail"

Our crime rate is far too high. Our level of cleanliness is frequently far too low. . . . We are often too loud and boisterous and spend far too much on drink. Even the most poverty-stricken among us can purchase a ten-cent bar of soap; even the most uneducated among us can have high morals.

—*STF* XI

So it was that, to the Negro, going to jail was no longer a disgrace but a badge of honor. The Revolution of the Negro not only attacked the external cause of his misery, but revealed him to himself. He was *somebody*.

—*WCW* II

Even where the polls are open to all, Negroes have shown themselves too slow to exercise their voting privileges. There must be a concerted effort on the part of Negro leaders to arouse their people from their apathetic indifference. . . . In the past, apathy was a moral failure. Today, it is a form of moral and political suicide.

—*STF* XI

One of the most damaging effects of past segregation on the personality of the Negro may well be that he has been victimized with the delusion that others should be more concerned than himself about his citizenship rights.

—*STF* XI

There are Negroes who will never fight for freedom. There are Negroes who will seek profit for themselves alone from the struggle. There are even some Negroes who will cooperate with their oppressors. . . . No one can pretend that because a people may be oppressed, every individual member is virtuous and worthy. The real issue is whether in the great mass the dominant characteristics are decency, honor, and courage.

—*WCW* II

. . . in avoiding the trap of domination by unworthy leaders, Negroes fell into the bog of political inactivity. They avoided victimization by any political group by withholding a significant commitment to any organization or individual.

—*WCW* VIII

The Negro is the child of two cultures—Africa and America. The problem is that in the search for wholeness all too many Negroes seek to embrace only one side of their natures.

—*WDWG* II

The American Negro is neither totally African nor totally Western. He is Afro-American, a true hybrid, a combination of two cultures.

—WDWG II

A hundred times I have been asked why we have allowed little children to march in demonstrations, to freeze and suffer in jails, to be exposed to bullets and dynamite. . . . Our families, as we have seen, are different. Oppression has again and again divided and splintered them. We are a people torn apart from era to era. It is logical, moral, and psychologically constructive for us to resist oppression united as families.

—WDWG IV

Only by being reconciled to ourselves will we be able to build upon the resources we already have at our disposal. Too many Negroes are jealous of other Negroes' successes and progress. Too many Negro organizations are warring against each other with a claim to absolute truth.

—WDWG IV

For any middle-class Negro to forget the masses is an act not only of neglect but of shameful ingratitude. It is time for the Negro haves to join hands with the Negro have-nots and, with compassion, journey into that other country of hurt and denial.

—WDWG IV

And so we shall have to do more than register and more than vote; we shall have to create leaders who embody virtues we can respect, who have moral and ethical principles we can applaud with enthusiasm.

—WDWG V

We have many assets to facilitate organization. Negroes are almost instinctively cohesive. We band together readily, and against white hostility we have an intense and wholesome loyalty to each other.

—*WDWG* V

PART TWO
THE MOVEMENT

MONTGOMERY

The majority of the Negroes who took part in the year-long boy-cott of Montgomery's buses were poor and untutored; but they understood the essence of the Montgomery movement; one elderly woman summed it up for the rest. When asked after several weeks of walking whether she was tired, she answered: "My feet is tired, but my soul is at rest."

—STF Preface

It is one of the splendid ironies of our day that Montgomery, the Cradle of the Confederacy, is being transformed into Montgomery, the cradle of freedom and justice.

—STF IV

There comes a time when people get tired of being plunged into the abyss of exploitation and nagging injustice. . . . But neither is this the whole explanation. Negroes in other communities confronted conditions equally as bad, and often worse. . . . Nor can it be explained by the appearance upon the scene of a new leadership. The Montgomery story would have taken place if the leaders of the protest had never been born. So every rational explanation breaks down at some point. There is something about the protest that is suprarational; it cannot be explained without a divine dimension.

—STF IV

I was in the kitchen drinking my coffee when I heard Coretta cry, "Martin, Martin, come quickly!" I put down my cup and ran toward the living room. As I approached the front window Coretta pointed joyfully to a slowly moving bus: "Darling, it's empty!" I could hardly believe what I saw. . . . Eagerly we waited for the next bus. In fifteen minutes it rolled down the street, and, like the first, it was empty.

—*STF* IV
December 5, 1955

If you will protest courageously, and yet with dignity and Christian love, when the history books are written in future generations, the historians will have to pause and say, "There lived a great people—a black people—who injected new meaning and dignity into the veins of civilization." This is our challenge and our overwhelming responsibility.

—*STF* IV
"Address to Holt Street Baptist Church"
December 5, 1955

"I must go back to Montgomery," I protested. "My friends and associates are being arrested. It would be the height of cowardice for me to stay away. I would rather be in jail ten years than desert my people now. I have begun the struggle, and I can't turn back. I have reached the point of no return."

—*STF* VIII
Atlanta, February 1956

I will always remember my delight when Mrs. Georgia Gilmore—an unlettered woman of unusual intelligence—told how an operator demanded that she get off the bus after paying her fare and board it again by the back door, and then drove away before she could get there. She turned to Judge Carter and said:

"When they count the money, they do not know Negro money from white money."

—*STF* VIII
March 1956

On that cloudy afternoon in March, Judge Carter had convicted more than Martin Luther King, Jr., Case No. 7399; he had convicted every Negro in Montgomery. It was no wonder that the movement couldn't be stopped. It was too large.

—*STF* VIII

That night the Ku Klux Klan rode. . . . My mail was warning that "if you allow the niggers to go back on the buses and sit in the front seats we're going to burn down fifty houses in one night, including yours."

—*STF* IX
Montgomery
November 1956

Ordinarily, threats of Klan action were a signal to the Negroes to go to their houses, close the doors, pull the shades or turn off the lights. . . . But this time they had prepared a surprise. . . . As the Klan drove by, the Negroes behaved as though they were watching a circus parade. Concealing the effort it cost them, many walked about as usual; some simply watched from their steps; a few waved at the passing cars. After a few blocks, the Klan, nonplussed, turned off into a side street and disappeared into the night.

—*STF* IX

In spite of all our efforts to prepare the Negroes for integrated buses, not a single white group would take the responsibility of preparing the white community.

—*STF* IX

As we go back to the buses let us be loving enough to turn an enemy into a friend. We must now move from protest to reconciliation.

—*STF* IX
December 20, 1956

As the white people boarded, many took seats as if nothing were going on. Others looked amazed to see Negroes sitting in front and some appeared peeved to know that they either had to sit behind the Negroes or stand.

—*STF* IX
First integrated bus ride
Montgomery
December 1956

A white woman unknowingly took a seat by a Negro. When she noticed her neighbor, she jumped up and said in a tone of obvious anger: "What are these niggers gonna do next?" But despite such signs of hostility, there were no major incidents.

—*STF* IX

. . . for the first time, I broke down in public. . . . Then, in the grip of an emotion I could not control, I said: "Lord, I hope no one will have to die as a result of our struggle for freedom in Montgomery. Certainly I don't want to die. But if anyone has to die, let it be me." The audience was in uproar. Shouts and cries of "no, no" came from all sides.

—*STF* IX
After the bombings in Montgomery
January 1957

But the diehards had made their last stand. The disturbances ceased abruptly. Desegregation on the buses proceeded smoothly. In a few weeks transportation was back to normal and people of both races rode together wherever they pleased. The skies did not fall when integrated buses finally travelled the streets of Montgomery.

—STF IX

Saturday nights are less belligerent than they used to be. There is a contagious spirit of friendliness and warmth; even the children seem to display a new sense of belonging.

—STF X

This growing self-respect has inspired the Negro with a new determination to struggle and sacrifice until first-class citizenship becomes a reality. This is the true meaning of the Montgomery story.

—STF X
1958

BIRMINGHAM

A nonviolent army has a magnificent universal quality. . . . In Birmingham, some of the most valued foot soldiers were youngsters ranging from elementary pupils to teenage high school and college students. . . . In Birmingham, the lame and the halt and the crippled could and did join up.

—*WCW* II

In Connor's Birmingham, the silent password was fear. It was a fear not only on the part of the black oppressed, but also in the hearts of the white oppressors. Guilt was a part of their fear.

—*WCW* III

In Birmingham, you would be living in a community where the white man's long-lived tyranny had cowed your people, led them to abandon hope, and developed in them a false sense of inferiority.

—*WCW* III

We are caught in an inescapable network of mutuality, tied in a single garment of destiny. Whatever affects one directly, affects all indirectly. Never again can we afford to live with the narrow, provincial "outside agitator" idea. . . . It is unfortunate that demonstrations are taking place in Birmingham, but it is even more unfortunate that the city's white power structure left the Negro community with no alternative.

—*WCW* V
"Letter from Birmingham Jail"
April 16, 1963

You [the eight fellow clergymen who had opposed the civil-rights action in Birmingham] warmly recommended the Birmingham police force for "keeping order" and "preventing violence." I doubt that you would have so warmly recommended the police force if you had seen its dogs sinking their teeth into unarmed, nonviolent Negroes . . . if you had seen them slap and kick old Negro men and young boys. . . .

—*WCW* V
"Letter from Birmingham Jail"

One of the most ringing replies came from a child of no more than eight who walked with her mother one day in a demonstration. An amused policeman leaned down to her and said with mock gruffness: "What do you want?" The child looked into his eyes, unafraid, and gave her answer. "F'eedom," she said. She could not even pronounce the word, but no Gabriel trumpet could have sounded a truer note.

—*WCW* VI
April 1963

Strangely enough, the masses of white citizens in Birmingham were not fighting us. . . . Only a year or so ago, Bull Connor would have had his job done for him by murderously angry white citizens. Now, however, the majority were maintaining a strictly hands-off policy.

—*WCW* VI
May 1963

Enraged, Bull Connor whirled on his men and shouted: "Dammit. Turn on the hoses." What happened in the next thirty seconds was one of the most fantastic events of the Birmingham story. . . . The marchers, many of them on their knees, stared back, unafraid and unmoving. Slowly the Negroes stood up and began to advance. Connor's men, as though hypnotized, fell back, their hoses sagging uselessly in their hands while several hundred Negroes marched past them, without further interference. . . .

—WCW VI
May 1963

The following day [May 1963], in an appropriate postscript, the Alabama Supreme Court ruled Eugene "Bull" Connor and his fellow commissioners out of office, once and for all. . . . I like to believe that Birmingham will one day become a model in southern race relations.

—WCW VI

The announcement that a peace pact had been signed in Birmingham was flashed across the world. . . . Segregationist forces within the city were consumed with fury. They vowed reprisals against the white businessmen who had "betrayed" them by capitulating to the cause of Negro equality. On Saturday night, they gave their brutal answer to the pact. Following a Ku Klux Klan meeting . . . the home of my brother . . . was bombed. That same night a bomb was planted near the Gaston Motel—in room 30—my room.

—WCW VI
May 1963

THE SUMMER OF 1963
(MARCH ON WASHINGTON)

Washington is a city of spectacles. . . . But in its entire glittering history, Washington had never seen a spectacle of the size and grandeur that assembled there on August 28, 1963.

—WCW VII

It was an army into which no one had to be drafted, it was white and Negro, and of all ages. . . . It was a fighting army, but no one should mistake that its most powerful weapon was love.

—WCW VII

Millions of white Americans, for the first time, had a clear, long look at Negroes engaged in a serious occupation. For the first time millions listened to the informed and thoughtful words of Negro spokesmen, from all walks of life. The stereotype of the Negro suffered a heavy blow.

—WCW VII

As television beamed the image of this extraordinary gathering across the border oceans, everyone who believed in man's capacity to better himself had a moment of inspiration and confidence in the future of the human race.

—WCW VII

In the bursting mood that has overtaken the Negro in 1963, the word "compromise" is profane and pernicious. The majority of Negro leadership is innately opposed to compromise.

—*WCW* VIII

Seen in perspective, the summer of 1963 was historic partly because it witnessed the first offensive in history launched by Negroes along a broad front. . . . And the virtues so long regarded as the exclusive property of the white South—gallantry, loyalty, and pride—had passed to the Negro demonstrators in the heat of the summer's battles.

—*WCW* VII

PART THREE
INSTITUTIONS

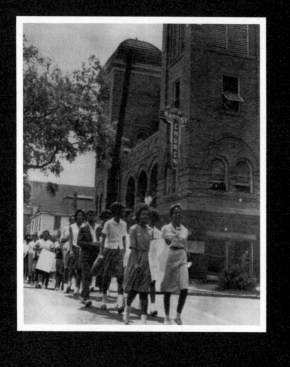

CHURCHES

The Church has an opportunity and duty to lift up its voice like a trumpet and declare unto the people the immorality of segregation. It must affirm that every human life is a reflection of divinity, and that every act of injustice mars and defaces the image of God in man.

—WDWG III

Colonialism could not have been perpetuated if the Christian Church had really taken a stand against it. One of the chief defenders of the vicious system of apartheid in South Africa is the Dutch Reformed Protestant Church.

—STL X

There are still too many Negro churches that are so absorbed in a future good "over yonder" that they condition their members to adjust to the present evils "over here."

—WDWG IV

So often the contemporary Church is a weak, ineffectual voice with an uncertain sound. So often it is an archdefender of the status quo.

—WCW V
"Letter from Birmingham Jail"

When I was suddenly catapulted into the leadership of the bus protest in Montgomery, Alabama, a few years ago, I felt we would be supported by the white Church. . . . Instead, some have been outright opponents, refusing to understand the freedom movement and misrepresenting its leaders; all too many others have been more cautious than courageous and have remained silent. . . .

—*WCW* V
"Letter from Birmingham Jail"

I am told that within American Protestantism there are more than two hundred and fifty denominations. The tragedy is not merely that you have such a multiplicity of denominations, but that many groups claim to possess absolute truth. . . . God is neither Baptist, Methodist, Presbyterian, or Episcopalian. God transcends our denominations.

—*STL* XIV
"Paul's Letter to American Christians"

If the Church does not participate actively in the struggle for peace and for economic and racial justice, it will forfeit the loyalty of millions and cause men everywhere to say that it has atrophied its will.

—*STL* VI

The judgment of God is upon the Church. The Church has a schism in its own soul that it must close. It will be one of the tragedies of Christian history if future historians record that at the height of the twentieth century the Church was one of the greatest bulwarks of white supremacy.

—*STL* X

The Church must be reminded that it is not the master or the servant of the state, but rather the conscience of the state. It must be the guide and the critic of the state, and never its tool.

—*STL* VI

During the last two world wars, national churches even functioned as the ready lackey of the state, sprinkling holy water upon the battleships and joining the mighty armies in singing "Praise the Lord and pass the ammunition." A weary world, pleading desperately for peace, has often found the Church morally sanctioning war.

—*STL* VI

If the Church is true to her mission, she must call for an end to the arms race.

—*STL* XV

Unfortunately, most of the major denominations still practice segregation in local churches, hospitals, schools, and other church institutions. It is appalling that the most segregated hour of Christian America is eleven o'clock on Sunday morning, the same hour when many are standing to sing: "In Christ There Is No East Nor West."

—*STF* X

Called to be the moral guardian of the community, the Church at times has preserved that which is immoral and unethical. Called to combat social evils, it has remained silent behind stained-glass windows.

—*STL* II

U.S. PRESIDENTS OF HIS DAY

. . . she [Coretta King] was denied even the consolation of a telephone call from her husband. . . . Remembering the call that John Kennedy had made to her during the 1960 election campaign, she placed a call to the president. Within a few minutes, his brother, Attorney General Robert Kennedy, phoned back. . . . A few hours later President Kennedy himself called Coretta from Palm Beach, and assured her he would look into the matter immediately. . . . After the president's intervention, conditions changed considerably.

—*WCW* IV
After King's arrest in Birmingham
1963

We were all involved in the death of John Kennedy. We tolerated hate; we tolerated the sick stimulation of violence in all walks of life; and we tolerated the differential application of law, which said that a man's life was sacred only if we agreed with his views.

—*WCW* VIII

No president except perhaps Lincoln had ever sufficiently given that degree of support to our struggle for freedom to justify our confidence. I had to conclude that the then known facts about Kennedy were not adequate to make an unqualified judgment in his favor. Today, I still believe that the civil rights movement must retain its independence. And yet, had President Kennedy lived, I would probably have endorsed him in the forthcoming election.

—*WCW* VIII
1964

His [Lyndon Johnson's] approach to the problem of civil rights was not identical with mine—nor had I expected it to be. Yet his careful practicality was nonetheless clearly no mask to conceal indifference. . . . Today, the dimensions of Johnson's leadership have spread from a region to a nation. His recent expressions, public and private, indicate that he has a comprehensive grasp of contemporary problems.

—*WCW* VIII
1963

. . . I do not doubt that the President [Johnson] is approaching the solution with sincerity, with realism and, thus far, with wisdom. . . . I will do everything in my power to make it so by outspoken agreement whenever proper, and determined opposition whenever necessary.

—*WCW* VIII

President Lyndon Johnson's high spirits were marked as he circulated among the many guests whom he had invited to witness an event he confidently felt to be historic, the signing of the 1965 Voting Rights Act. . . . The bill that lay on the polished mahogany desk was born in violence in Selma, Alabama, where a stubborn sheriff . . . had stumbled against the future.

—*WDWG* I

U.S. COURTS

This decision [the *Brown* v. *Board of Education* Supreme Court ruling of 1954] is a great beacon-light of hope to millions of disinherited people. Looking back, we see the forces of segregation gradually dying on the seashore. . . . At least we have left Egypt, and with patient yet firm determination we shall reach the promised land.

—STL VIII

Today we are witnessing a massive change. A world-shaking decree by the nine justices of the United States Supreme Court [of 1954] opened the Red Sea and the forces of justice are moving to the other side. The Court affirmed that separate facilities are inherently unequal. . . .

—STL VIII

Another letter cursed the Supreme Court and threatened "that damned Hugo Black: When he comes to Alabama we're going to hang you and him from the same tree."

—STF IX

. . . with a mixture of anxiety and hope, I read these words: "The United States Supreme Court today affirmed a decision of a . . . District Court in declaring Alabama's state and local laws requiring segregation on buses unconstitutional." . . . At this moment my heart began to throb with an inexpressible joy. The darkest hour of our struggle had indeed proved to be the hour of victory.

—*STF* IX
November 13, 1956

But the courts are no longer so certain of their role. They remember too well what happened to their rulings on bus segregation. . . . They fear that the high Court could also knock out other forms of segregation in public facilities.

—*STF* X

When the Supreme Court decision on school desegregation was handed down, leading segregationists vowed to thwart it by invoking "a century of litigation" . . . The injunction method has now become the leading instrument of the South to block the direct-action civil-rights drive. . . . The Alabama courts are notorious for "sitting on" cases of this nature. . . . When the injunction was issued in Birmingham, our failure to obey bewildered our opponents. . . . I intended to be one of the first to see the example of civil disobedience.

—*WCW* IV

. . . It would be a mistake to minimize the impact upon the South of the federal court orders and legislative and executive acts already in effect. Federal court decrees have altered transportation patterns, teachers' salaries, the use of recreational facilities, and myriad of other matters.

—*STF* X

LABOR UNIONS

The unions forming the AFL-CIO include 1.3 million Negroes among their 13.5 million members. Only the combined religious institutions serving the Negro community can claim a greater membership of Negroes. The Negro then has a right to expect the resources of the American trade union movement to be used in assuring him—like all the rest of its members—of a proper place in American society.

—STF XI

In unhappy contrast, the National Council of the AFL-CIO declined to support the March [on Washington, August 1963] and adopted a position of neutrality. A number of international unions, however, independently declared their support. . . .

—WCW VII

It is interesting to note that some of the states that today are opposing progress in civil rights were the same that defied the union's efforts during the thirties.

—WCW VIII

Negroes battling for their own recognition today have a right to expect more from their old allies. Nothing would hold back the forces of progress in American life more effectively than a schism between the Negro and organized labor.

—WCW VIII

To play our role fully as Negroes we will have to strive for en-
hanced representation and influence in the labor movement. Our
young people need to think of union careers as earnestly as they
do of business careers and professions.

—*WDWG* V

SCHOOLS

. . . we are now [1966] able to see why the Supreme Court decision on school desegregation, which we described at the time as historic, has not made history. After twelve years, barely 12 percent school desegregation existed in the whole South, and in the Deep South the figure hardly reached 2 percent. And even these few schools were in many cases integrated only with a handful of Negroes.

—WDWG I

In elementary schools Negroes lag one to three years behind whites, and their segregated schools receive substantially less money per student than do the white schools.

—WDWG I

Crises arising in Northern schools are interpreted as proofs that Negroes are inherently delinquent. The extremists do not recognize that these school problems are symptoms of urban dislocation, rather than expressions of racial deficiency.

—STF XI

The schools of the South are the present storm center. Here the forces that stand for the best in our national life have been tragically ineffectual . . . the forces of goodwill failed to come through. The Office of the President was appallingly silent. . . . Other forces of justice also failed to act.

—STF XI

PART FOUR
PHILOSOPHIES

GANDHI

Then I was introduced to the life and teachings of Mahatma Gandhi. As I read his works I became deeply fascinated by his campaigns of nonviolent resistance.

—STL XV

Christ furnished the spirit and motivation, while Gandhi furnished the method.

—STF V

As the days unfolded, however, the inspiration of Mahatma Gandhi began to exert its influence. I had come to see early that the Christian doctrine of love operating through the Gandhian method of nonviolence was one of the most potent weapons available to the Negro in his struggle for freedom.

—STF V

For more than twenty years Mahatma Gandhi unrelentingly urged British viceroys, governors, generals, prime ministers, and kings to let his people go. Like the pharaohs of old, the British leaders turned deaf ears to these agonizing pleas.

—STL VIII

If he [the black man] has to go to jail for the cause of freedom, let him enter it in the fashion Gandhi urged his countrymen, "as the bridegroom enters the bride's chamber"—that is, with a little trepidation but with a great expectation.

—*STF* XI

. . . it must be emphasized that nonviolent resistance is not a method for cowards; it does resist. If one uses this method because he is afraid or merely because he lacks the instruments of violence, he is not truly nonviolent. This is why Gandhi often said that if cowardice is the only alternative to violence, it is better to fight.

—*STF* VI

After struggling for years to achieve independence, Mahatma Gandhi witnessed a bloody religious war between the Hindus and the Moslems, and the subsequent division of India and Pakistan shattered his heart's desire for a united nation. Woodrow Wilson died before realizing the fulfillment of his consuming vision of a League of Nations. . . . Shattered dreams are the hallmark of our mortal life.

—*STL* IX

COMMUNISM

First I rejected their materialistic interpretation of history. Communism, avowedly secularistic and materialistic, has no place for God. . . . Second, I strongly disagreed with communism's ethical relativism. . . . Almost anything—force, violence, murder, lying—is a justifiable means to the "millenial" end. . . . Third, I opposed communism's political totalitarianism. In communism, the individual ends up in subjection to the state.

—*STF* VI
Reading Marx
December 1949

My reading of Marx also convinced me that truth is found neither in Marxism nor in the traditional capitalism. Each represents a partial truth. Historically, capitalism failed to see the truth in collective enterprise and Marxism failed to see the truth in individual enterprise.

—*STF* VI

Nothing provides the Communists with a better climate for expansion and infiltration than the continued alliance of our nation with racism and exploitation throughout the world.

—*WDWG* VI

Capitalism may lead to a practical materialism that is as pernicious as the theoretical materialism taught by communism. We must honestly recognize that truth is not to be found either in traditional capitalism or in Marxism.

—STL X

We must not call everyone a Communist or an appeaser who recognizes that hate and hysteria are not the final answers to the problems of these turbulent days. We must not engage in a nega-tive anticommunism, but rather in a positive thrust for de-mocracy.

—STL X

There is a convenient temptation to attribute the current tur-moil and bitterness throughout the world to the presence of a Communist conspiracy to undermine Europe and America, but the potential explosiveness of our world situation is much more attributable to disillusionment with promises of Christianity and technology.

—WDWG VI

It is a sad fact that, because of comfort, complacency, a morbid fear of communism, and our proneness to adjust to injustice, the Western nations that initiated so much of the revolutionary spirit of the modern world have now become the arch-antirevo-lutionaries. . . . Communism is a judgment on our failure to make democracy real and to follow through on the revolutions that we initiated.

—WDWG VI

LIBERALS AND CONSERVATIVES

Liberalism provided me with an intellectual satisfaction that I never found in fundamentalism. I became so enamored of the insights of liberalism that I almost fell into the trap of accepting uncritically everything it encompassed.

—STL XV

For years now I have heard the word "Wait!" It rings in the ear of every Negro with piercing familiarity. This "Wait" has almost always meant "Never."

—WCW V
"Letter from Birmingham Jail"

While I saw neo-orthodoxy as a helpful corrective for a sentimental liberalism, I felt that it did not provide an adequate answer to basic questions. . . . Neo-orthodoxy fell into a mood of antirationalism and semifundamentalism, stressing a narrow, uncritical biblicism.

—STL XV

I realized that liberalism has been all too sentimental concerning human nature and that it leaned toward a false idealism. . . . Liberalism failed to show that reason by itself is little more than an instrument to justify man's defensive ways of thinking. Reason, devoid of the purifying power of faith, can never free itself from distortions and rationalizations.

—STL XV

Today in all too many Northern communities a sort of quasi liberalism prevails, so bent on seeing all sides that it fails to become dedicated to any side. . . . A true liberal will not be deterred by the propaganda and subtle words of those who say, "Slow up for a while; you are pushing things too fast."

—STF X

I have almost reached the regrettable conclusion that the Negro's great stumbling block in his stride toward freedom is not the White Citizen's Counciler or the Ku Klux Klanner, but the white moderate, who is more devoted to "order" than to justice.

—WCW V
"Letter from Birmingham Jail"

When the Negro was completely an underdog, he needed white spokesmen. Liberals played their parts in this period exceedingly well. . . . But now that the Negro has rejected his role as an underdog, he has become more assertive in his search for identity and group solidarity; he wants to speak for himself.

—WDWG III

The conservatives who say, "Let us not move so fast," and the extremists who say, "Let us go out and whip the world," would tell you that they are as far apart as the poles. But there is a striking parallel: They accomplish nothing; for they do not reach the people who have a crying need to be free.

—WCW II

THE PRINCIPLE OF NONVIOLENCE

From the beginning a basic philosophy guided the movement. This guiding principle has since been referred to variously as nonviolent resistance, noncooperation, and passive resistance. But in the first days of the protest none of these expressions was mentioned; the phrase most often heard was "Christian love."

—STF V

Admittedly, nonviolence in the truest sense is not a strategy that one uses simply because it is expedient at the moment; nonviolence is ultimately a way of life that men live by because of the sheer morality of its claim.

—STF V

A second basic fact that characterizes nonviolence is that it does not seek to defeat or humiliate the opponent, but to win his friendship and understanding.

—STF VI

A fifth point concerning nonviolent resistance is that it avoids not only external physical violence but also internal violence of spirit. The nonviolent resister not only refuses to shoot his opponent but he also refuses to hate him.

—STF VI

A sixth basic fact about nonviolent resistance is that it is based on the conviction that the universe is on the side of justice. Consequently, the believer in nonviolence has deep faith in the future.

—STF VI

Nonviolent resistance makes it possible for the Negro to remain in the South and struggle for his rights. The Negro's problem will not be solved by running away.

—STF XI

If the American Negro and other victims of oppression succumb to the temptation of using violence in the struggle for freedom, future generations will be the recipients of a desolate night of bitterness, and our chief legacy to them will be an endless reign of meaningless chaos.

—STF XI

. . . we urged the volunteers to give up any possible weapons they might have on their persons. Hundreds of people responded to this appeal. Some of them carried penknives . . . not because they wanted to use them against the police, but because they wanted to defend themselves against Mr. Connor's dogs. We proved to them that we needed no weapons—not so much as a toothpick.

—WCW IV
Birmingham
April 1963

We did not hesitate to call our movement an army. But it was a special army, with no supplies but its sincerity, no uniform but its determination, no arsenal except its faith, no currency but its conscience.

—WCW IV

You [the eight fellow clergymen who opposed the civil rights action] are quite right in calling for negotiation. Indeed, this is the very purpose of direct action. Nonviolent direct action seeks to create such a crisis and foster such a tension that a community which has constantly refused to negotiate is forced to confront the issue.

—*WCW* V
"Letter from Birmingham Jail"

Some few spectators, who had not been trained in the discipline of nonviolence, reacted to the brutality of the policemen by throwing rocks and bottles. But the demonstrators remained nonviolent. In the face of this resolution and bravery, the moral conscience of the nation was deeply stirred. . . .

—*WCW* VI
Birmingham
May 4, 1963

They tried to stop us by threats and fear, the tactic that had long worked so effectively. But nonviolence had muzzled their guns and Negro defiance had shaken their confidence. When they finally reached for clubs, dogs, and guns, they found the world was watching, and then the power of nonviolent protest became manifest.

—*TOC* I

I am still convinced that a solution of nonviolence remains possible. However, nonviolence must be adapted to urban conditions and urban moods. . . . In the South, a march was a social earthquake; in the North, it is a faint, brief exclamation of protest.

—*TOC* I

I am convinced that even very violent temperaments can be channeled through nonviolent discipline, if the movement is moving, if they can act constructively and express through an effective channel their very legitimate anger.

—*TOC* IV

I am only too well aware of the human weakness and failures which exist, the doubts of the efficacy of nonviolence, and the open advocacy of violence by some. But I am still convinced that nonviolence is still the most practically sound and morally excellent way to grapple with the age-old problem of racial injustice.

—NL

In a world facing the revolt of ragged and hungry masses of God's children; in a world torn between the tensions of East and West, white and colored, individualists and collectivists. . . . In this world, nonviolence is no longer an option for intellectual analysts, it is an imperative for action.

—*TOC* IV

SEGREGATION

When the white man argues that segregation should continue because of the Negro's lagging standards, he fails to see that the standards lag because of segregation.

—*STF* XI

Even the most casual observer can see that the South has marvelous possibilities. It is rich in natural resources, blessed with the beauties of nature and endowed with a native warmth of spirit. Yet in spite of these assets, it is retarded by a blight that debilitates not only the Negro but also the white man. . . . Segregation has placed the whole South socially, educationally, and economically behind the rest of the nation.

—*STF* XI

The enemies of racial progress . . . would delight in believing that there is chaos up front in the civil-rights ranks. The hard truth is that the unity of the movement is a remarkable feature of major importance. The fact that different organizations place various degrees of emphasis on certain tactical approaches is not indicative of disunity. Unity has never meant uniformity.

—*WCW* VIII

Just as the Congress passed a civil rights bill in 1868 and refused to enforce it, the Congress passed a civil rights bill in 1964 and

to this day has failed to enforce it in all its dimensions.
—*WDWG* III
1967

Some people feel that their attempt to preserve segregation is best for themselves, their children, and their nation. . . . Pressed for a religious vindication for their conviction, they will even argue that God was the first segregationist. "Red birds and blue birds don't fly together," they contend. . . . They do not know, or they refuse to know, that the idea of an inferior race has been refuted by the best evidence of the science of anthropology.
—*STL* IV

The two elements that are still most responsible for active segregationist sentiment are the newspapers and the politicians. Day in and day out the press is filled with stories of racial conflict. . . . Likewise the editorial pages constantly hammer at the Negro question. Readers are never permitted to forget that there is a war against "Yankees and race mixing."
—*STF* X

While abhorring segregation, we shall love the segregationist. This is the only way to create the beloved community.
—*STL* V

Today we know with certainty that segregation is dead. The only question remaining is how costly will be the funeral.
—*STL* XI

JUSTICE AND INJUSTICE

I had also learned that the inseparable twin of racial injustice was economic injustice. Although I came from a home of economic security and relative comfort, I could never get out of my mind the economic insecurity of many of my playmates and the tragic poverty of those living around me.

—STF VI

As I like to say to the people in Montgomery: "The tension in this city is not between white people and Negro people. The tension is, at bottom, between justice and injustice, between the forces of light and the forces of darkness."

—STF VI

There is such a thing as the freedom of exhaustion. Some people are so worn down by the yoke of oppression that they give up. . . . The oppressed must never allow the conscience of the oppressor to slumber. . . . To accept injustice or segregation passively is to say to the oppressor that his actions are morally right.

—STF XI

We must pray with unceasing passion for racial justice, but we must also use our minds to develop a programme . . . to bring an end to racial injustice.

—STL XIII

One has not only a legal but a moral responsibility to obey just laws. Conversely, one has a moral responsibility to disobey unjust laws.

—*WCW* V
"Letter from Birmingham Jail"

A law is unjust if it is inflicted on a minority that, as a result of being denied the right to vote, had no part in enacting or devising the law. Who can say that the legislature of Alabama which set up the state's segregation laws was democratically elected?

—*WCW* V
"Letter from Birmingham Jail"

I submit that an individual who breaks a law that conscience tells him is unjust, and is willing to accept the penalty of imprisonment in order to arouse the conscience of the community over its injustice, is in reality expressing the highest respect for the law.

—*WCW* V
"Letter from Birmingham Jail"

We should never forget that everything Adolf Hitler did in Germany was "legal" and everything the Hungarian freedom fighters did in Hungary was "illegal."

—*WCW* V
"Letter from Birmingham Jail"

Power at its best is love implementing the demands of justice. Justice at its best is love correcting everything that stands against love.

—*WDWG* II

GOOD AND EVIL

Without love, benevolence becomes egotism and martyrdom becomes spiritual pride.

—*STL* XIV

The soft-minded man always fears change. He feels security in the status quo, and he has an almost morbid fear of the new. For him, the greatest pain is the pain of a new idea.

—*STL* I

Many modern men . . . contend, as did Rousseau, that human nature is essentially good. Evil is to be found only in institutions, and if poverty and ignorance were to be removed everything would be all right. The twentieth century opened with a glowing optimism.

—*STL* VII

We have learned to fly the air like birds and swim the sea like fish, but we have not learned the simple art of living together as brothers. Our abundance has brought us neither peace of mind nor serenity of spirit.

—*STL* VII

I am convinced that the universe is under the control of a loving purpose, and that in the struggle for righteousness man has cosmic companionship. Behind the harsh appearance of the world there is a benign power.

—*STL* XV

Why does not God break in and smash the evil schemes of wicked men? . . . By endowing us with freedom, God relinquished a measure of his own sovereignty and imposed certain limitations upon himself. If his children are free, they must do his will by a voluntary choice.

—*STL* VIII

Death is not the ultimate evil; the ultimate evil is to be outside God's love. We need not join the mad rush to purchase an earthly fallout shelter. God is our eternal fallout shelter.

—*STL* XII

The Renaissance was too optimistic, and the Reformation too pessimistic. The former so concentrated on the goodness of man that it overlooked his capacity for evil; the latter so concentrated on the wickedness of man that it overlooked his capacity for goodness.

—*STL* XIII

The real weakness of the idea that God will do everything is its false conception of both God and man. It makes God so absolutely sovereign that man is absolutely helpless. . . . This view ends up with a God who is a despot and not a Father.

—*STL* XIII

CHRISTIAN FAITH

Religion operates not only on the vertical plane but also on the horizontal. It seeks not only to integrate men with God but to integrate men with men and each man with himself. This means, at bottom, that the Christian gospel is a two-way road; on the one hand it seeks to change the souls of men, and thereby unite them with God; on the other hand it seeks to change the environmental conditions of men so that the soul will have a chance after it is changed.

—*STF* I

We talk eloquently about our commitment to the principles of Christianity, and yet our lives are saturated with the practices of paganism. We proclaim our devotion to democracy, but we sadly practice the very opposite of the democratic creed. . . . This strange dichotomy, this agonizing gulf between the *ought* and the *is*, represents the tragic theme of man's earthly pilgrimage.

—*STL* IV

The Christian faith makes it possible for us nobly to accept that which cannot be changed, and to meet disappointments and sorrow with an inner poise, and to absorb the most intense pain without abandoning our sense of hope. . . .

—*STL* IX

I would be the last to condemn the thousands of sincere and dedicated people outside the churches who have labored unselfishly through various humanitarian movements to cure the world of social evils, for I would rather a man be a committed humanist than an uncommitted Christian.

—STL XIII

Christianity clearly affirms that in the long struggle between good and evil, good eventually will emerge as victor. . . . Good Friday must give way to the triumphant music of Easter.

—STL VIII

Abnormal fears and phobias that are expressed in neurotic anxiety may be cured by psychiatry; but the fear of death, nonbeing, and nothingness, expressed in existential anxiety, may be cured only by a positive religious faith.

—STL XII

This lopsided Reformation theology has often emphasized a purely otherworldly religion, which stresses the utter hopelessness of this world and calls upon the individual to concentrate on preparing his soul for the world to come. By ignoring the need for social reform, religion is divorced from the mainstream of human life.

—STL XIII

This faith [in God] transforms the whirlwind of despair into a warm and reviving breeze of hope. The words of a motto which generations ago were commonly found on the wall in the homes of devout persons need to be etched in our hearts:

> Fear knocked at the door.
> Faith answered.
> There was no one there.

—STL XII

LOVE AND COMPASSION

Tough-mindedness without tenderheartedness is cold and detached, leaving one's life in a perpetual winter devoid of the warmth of spring and the gentle heat of summer.

—STL I

The hard-hearted individual never sees people as people, but rather as mere objects or as impersonal cogs in an ever-turning wheel. In the vast wheel of industry, he sees men as hands.

—STL I

When our most tireless efforts fail to stop the surging sweep of oppression, we need to know that in this universe is a God whose matchless strength is a fit contrast to the sordid weakness of man. But there are also times when we need to know that God possesses love and mercy.

—STL I

Desegregation will break down the legal barriers and bring men together physically, but something must touch the hearts and souls of men so that they will come together spiritually because it is natural and right.

—STL III

One day we will learn that the heart can never be totally right
if the head is totally wrong. Only through the bringing together
of head and heart—intelligence and goodness—shall man rise to
a fulfillment of his true nature.

—*STL* IV

Probably no admonition has been more difficult to follow than
Jesus' command to "love your enemies." Some men have sincerely felt that its actual practice is not possible. . . . Jesus, they
say, was an impractical idealist.

—*STL* V

. . . we must recognize that the evil deed of the enemy-
neighbour, the thing that hurts, never quite expresses all that
he is. An element of goodness may be found even in our worst
enemy. Each of us is something of a schizophrenic personality,
tragically divided against ourselves.

—*STL* V

Darkness cannot drive out darkness; only light can do that. Hate
cannot drive out hate; only love can do that. . . . The chain
reaction of evil—hate begetting hate, wars producing more
wars—must be broken, or we shall be plunged into the abyss of
annihilation.

—*STL* V

Everybody wishes to love and to be loved. He who feels that he
is not loved feels that he does not count. Much has happened
in the modern world to make men feel that they do not belong.

—*STL* VI

The hard-core hippie is a remarkable contradiction. He uses
drugs to turn inward, away from reality, to find peace and secu-

rity. Yet he advocates love as the highest human value—love, which can exist only in communication between people, and not in the total isolation of the individual.

—*TOC* III

Somehow we must be able to stand up before our most bitter opponents and say: "We shall match your capacity to inflict suffering by our capacity to endure suffering. We will meet your physical force with soul force. Do to us what you will and we will still love you."

—*TOC* V

"I" cannot reach fulfillment without "thou." The self cannot be self without other selves. Self-concern without other-concern is like a tributary that has no outward flow to the ocean.

—*WDWG* VI

The oceans of history are made turbulent by the ever-rising tides of hate. History is cluttered with the wreckage of nations and individuals that pursued that self-defeating path of hate. Love is the key to the solution of the problems of the world.

—NL

PART FIVE
ISSUES

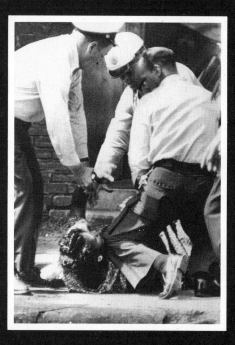

RACISM

We see men as Jews or Gentiles, Catholics or Protestants, Chinese or American, Negroes or whites. We fail to think of them as fellow human beings made from the same basic stuff as we, moulded in the same divine image.

—*STL* III

One of the great tragedies of man's long trek along the highway of history has been the limiting of our neighbourly concern to tribe, race, class, or nation. The God of early Old Testament days was a tribal god and the ethic was tribal. "Thou shalt not kill" meant "Thou shalt not kill a fellow Israelite, but for God's sake, kill a Philistine." Greek democracy embraced a certain aristocracy, but not the hordes of Greek slaves. . . .

—*STL* III

Since before the Civil War, the alliance of Southern racism and Northern reaction has been the major roadblock to all social advancement. . . . This explains why the United States is still far behind European nations in all forms of social legislation.

—*WDWG* I

Racism is a philosophy based on a contempt for life. It is the arrogant assertion that one race is the center of value and object of devotion, before which other races must kneel in submission. . . . Racism is total estrangement.

—*WDWG* III

Every Negro comes face to face with this color shock, and it constitutes a major emotional crisis. . . . All prejudice is evil, but the prejudice that rejects a man because of the color of his skin is the most despicable expression of man's inhumanity to man.

—*WDWG* IV

Nothing today more clearly indicates the residue of racism still lodging in our society than the responses of white America to integrated housing. Here the tides of prejudice, fear, and irrationality rise to flood proportions.

—*WDWG* IV

The fact that professional white hoodlums and racketeers are located in the best neighborhoods of Cicero is fit proof that the opposition to open housing is not based on behavior or moral standards. The reason that Ralph Bunche could not live in Cicero is that he is a Negro, pure and simple. His individual culture, brilliance, and character are not considered.

—*WDWG* IV

Among the moral imperatives of our time, we are challenged to work all over the world with unshakable determination to wipe out the last vestiges of racism. . . . Racism is no mere American phenomenon. Its vicious grasp knows no geographical boundaries.

—*WDWG* VI

If Western civilization does not now respond constructively to the challenge to banish racism, some future historian will have to say that a great civilization died because it lacked the soul and commitment to make justice a reality for all men.

—*WDWG* VI

AMERICAN MINORITIES

Our children are still taught to respect the violence which reduced a red-skinned people of an earlier culture into a few frag-
mented groups herded into impoverished reservations. This is in
sharp contrast to many nations south of the border, which assim-
ilated their Indians, respected their culture, and elevated many
of them to high position.

—*WCW* VII

The bravery of the Indian, employing spears and arrows against
the Winchester and the Colt, had ultimately to eventuate in
defeat. On the other hand . . . nonresistance merely reinforces
the myth that one race is inferior to another. Negroes today are
neither exercising violence nor accepting domination.

—*WCW* VII

Few other minority groups have maintained a political aloofness
and a nonpartisan posture as rigidly and as long as Negroes. The
Germans, Irish, Italians, and Jews, after a period of acclimatiza-
tion, moved inside political formations and exercised influence.
Negroes, partly by choice but substantially by exclusion, have
operated outside of the political structures. . . .

—*WCW* VIII

No one has ever heard the Jews publicly chant a slogan of Jewish
power, but they have power. Through group unity, determina-

tion, and creative endeavor, they have gained it. The same thing is true of Irish or Italian power. Neither group has used a slogan of Irish or Italian power, but they worked hard to achieve it. This is exactly what we must do.

—WDWG II

In a multiracial society no group can make it alone. It is a myth to believe that the Irish, Italians, and the Jews . . . rose to power through separatism. . . . Their group unity was always enlarged by joining in alliances with other groups such as political machines and trade unions.

—WDWG II

Negroes nurture a persistent myth that the Jews of America attained social mobility and status solely because they had money. It is unwise to ignore the error for many reasons. In a negative sense it encourages anti-Semitism and overestimates money as a value. In a positive sense the full truth reveals a useful lesson. Jews progressed because they possessed a tradition of education combined with social and political action.

—WDWG V

It would be a tragic and immoral mistake to identify the mass of Negroes with the very small number that succumb to cheap and dishonest [anti-Semitic] slogans, just as it would be a serious error to identify all Jews with the few who exploit Negroes under their economic sway.

—WDWG III

Other immigrant groups came to America with language and economic handicaps, but not with the stigma of color. Above all, no other ethnic group has been a slave on American soil, and no other group has had its family structure deliberately torn apart. This is the rub.

—*WDWG* IV

The future of the deep structural changes we seek will not be found in the decaying political machines. It lies in new alliances of Negroes, Puerto Ricans, Labor, Liberals, certain Church and middle-class elements.

—*WDWG* V

POVERTY

When the locomotive of history roared through the nineteenth century and the first half of the twentieth, it left the nation's black masses standing forlornly at dismal terminals. . . . The scientific achievements of today, particularly the explosive advance of automation, may be blessings to our economy, but for the Negro they are a curse. . . . The livelihood of millions has dwindled down . . . because the unskilled and semiskilled jobs they filled have disappeared under the magic of automation.

—*WCW* VIII

The Negro today is not struggling for some abstract, vague rights, but for concrete improvement in his way of life. What will it profit him to be able to send his children to an integrated school if the family income is insufficient to buy them school clothes?

—*WCW* VIII

The misery of the poor in Africa and Asia is shared misery, a fact of life for the vast majority; they are all poor together as a result of years of exploitation and underdevelopment. In sad contrast, the poor in America know that they live in the richest nation in the world. . . .

—NL

The poor in our countries have been shut out of our minds and driven from the mainstream of our societies, because we have allowed them to become invisible.

—NL

Without denying the value of scientific endeavor, there is a striking absurdity in committing billions to reach the moon where no people live, while only a fraction of that amount is appropriated to service the densely populated slums.

—*WDWG* III

The Peace Corps will fail if it seeks to do something *for* the underprivileged people of the world; it will succeed if it seeks creatively to do something *with* them. It will fail as a negative gesture to defeat communism: it will succeed only as a positive effort to wipe poverty, ignorance, and disease from the earth.

—*STL* III

But while so many white Americans are unaware of conditions inside the ghetto, there are very few ghetto dwellers who are unaware of the life outside. The television sets bombard them day by day with the opulence of the larger society.

—*WDWG* IV

Contrary to the myth held by many white Americans, the ghetto is not a monolithic unit of dope addicts, alcoholics, prostitutes, and unwed mothers. There are churches in the ghetto as well as bars.

—*WDWG* IV

Consumer items range from five to twelve cents higher in the ghetto stores than in the suburban stores, both run by the same supermarket chains. . . . This exploitation is possible because so many residents of the ghetto have no personal means of transportation.

—*WDWG* IV

It is a simple matter of justice that America, in dealing creatively with the task of raising the Negro from backwardness, should also be rescuing a large stratum of the forgotten white poor. A Bill of Rights for the Disadvantaged could mark the rise of a new era. . . .

—*WCW* VIII

I am now convinced that the simplest approach will prove to be the most effective—the solution to poverty is to abolish it directly by a now widely discussed measure: the guaranteed income.

—*WDWG* V

The dignity of the individual will flourish when the decisions concerning his life are in his own hands, when he has the assurance that his income is stable and certain, and when he knows that he has the means to seek self-improvement.

—*WDWG* V

The program [of guaranteed income] would benefit all the poor, including the two-thirds of them who are white. I hope that both Negro and white will act in coalition to effect this change, because their combined strength will be necessary to overcome the fierce opposition we must realistically anticipate.

—*WDWG* V

The curse of poverty has no justification in our age. It is socially as cruel and blind as the practice of cannibalism at the dawn of civilization, when men ate each other because they had not yet learned to take food from the soil or to consume the abundant animal life around them. The time has come for us to civilize ourselves by the total, direct, and immediate abolition of poverty.

—*WDWG* V

Jesus never made a sweeping indictment against wealth. Rather, he condemned the misuse of wealth. Money, like any other force such as electricity, is amoral and can be used for either good or evil.

—*STL* VII

CONFORMITY

Many people fear nothing more terribly than to take a position which stands out sharply and clearly from the prevailing opinion. The tendency of most is to adopt a view that is so ambiguous that it will include everything and so popular that it will include everybody.

—*STL* II

Success, recognition, and conformity are the bywords of the modern world where everyone seems to crave the anesthetizing security of being identified with the majority.

—*STL* II

Not a few men who cherish lofty and noble ideals hide them under a bushel for fear of being called different. Many sincere people in the South privately oppose segregation and discrimination, but they are apprehensive lest they be publicly condemned.

—*STL* II

Millions of citizens are deeply disturbed that the military-industrial complex too often shapes national policy, but they do not want to be considered unpatriotic.

—*STL* II

We are called to be people of conviction, not conformity; of moral nobility, not social respectability. We are commanded to live differently and according to a higher loyalty.

—*STL* II

A legion of thoughtful persons recognizes that traditional capitalism must continually undergo change if our great national wealth is to be more equitably distributed, but they are afraid their criticism will make them seem un-American.

—*STL* II

Blind conformity makes us so suspicious of an individual who insists on saying what he really believes that we recklessly threaten his civil liberties. . . . If a Southern white person, believing in the American dream of the dignity and worth of human personality, dares to invite a Negro into his home and join with him in his struggle for freedom, he is liable to be summoned before some legislative investigation body. He most certainly is a Communist if he espouses the cause of human brotherhood!

—*STL* II

If Americans permit thought-control, business-control, and freedom-control to continue, we shall surely move within the shadows of fascism.

—*STL* II

The trailblazers in human, academic, scientific, and religious freedom have always been nonconformists. In any cause that concerns the progress of mankind, put your faith in the nonconformist!

—*STL* II

Will we march only to the music of time, or will we, risking criticism and abuse, march to the soul-saving music of eternity?

—*STL* II

WHITE BACKLASH

On the national scene, the Congress today is dominated by southern reactionaries whose control of the key committees enables them to determine legislation. Disenfranchisement of the Negro and the nonexercise of the vote by poor whites have permitted the southern congressman to wrest his election from a tiny group, which he manipulates easily to return him again and again to office.

—WCW VIII

But the Southern States have made their policy clear. States' rights, they say in effect, include the right to abrogate power when it involves distasteful responsibilities, even to the Constitution of the United States. . . . So the power and the responsibility return by default to the federal government.

—STF XI

A year later, some of the Negro leaders who had been present in Selma and the Capitol ceremonies no longer held office in their organizations. They had been discarded to symbolize a radical change of tactics. A year later, the white backlash had become an emotional electoral issue in California, Maryland, and elsewhere.

—*WDWG* I
1967

White America was ready to demand that the Negro should be spared the lash of brutality and coarse degradation, but had never been truly committed to helping him out of poverty, exploitation, or all forms of discrimination.

—*WDWG* I

When Negroes looked for the second phase, the realization of equality, they found that many of their white allies had quietly disappeared. . . . To stay murder is not the same thing as to ordain brotherhood.

—*WDWG* I

The inevitable counterrevolution that succeeds every period of progress is taking place. Failing to understand this as a normal process of development, some Negroes are falling into unjustified pessimism and despair.

—*WDWG* I

Laws that affect the whole population—draft laws, income-tax laws, traffic laws—manage to work even though they may be unpopular, but laws passed for the Negro's benefit are so widely unenforced that it is a mockery to call them laws.

—*WDWG* III

There will be agonizing setbacks along with creative advances. Our consolation is that no one can know the true taste of victory if he has never swallowed defeat.

—*WDWG* V

The decade of 1955 to 1965 with its constructive elements mis-led us. Everyone underestimated the amount of violence and rage Negroes were suppressing and the amount of bigotry the white majority was disguising.

—*TOC* I

BLACK POWER

. . . I am further convinced that if our white brothers dismiss as "rabble-rousers" and "outside agitators" those of us who employ nonviolent direct action . . . millions of Negroes will, out of frustration and despair, seek solace and security in black-national ideologies—a development that would inevitably lead to a frightening racial nightmare.

—WCW V
"Letter from Birmingham Jail"

The Negro has many pent-up resentments and latent frustrations, and he must release them. So let him march; let him make prayer pilgrimages to the city hall; let him go on freedom rides. . . . If his repressed emotions are not released in nonviolent ways, they will seek expression through violence.

—WCW V
"Letter from Birmingham Jail"

In the past year, nonviolent direct action has been pronounced for the tenth time dead. New tactics have been proposed to replace it. . . . Yet Black Power has proved to be a slogan without a program, and with an uncertain following.

—WDWG I
1967

For people who had been crushed so long by white power and who had been taught that black was degrading, it [the Black

Power slogan] had a ready appeal. Immediately, however, I had reservations about its use. I had the deep feeling that it was an unfortunate choice of words for a slogan.

—*WDWG* II

It is no accident that the birth of this slogan [Black Power] in the civil rights movement took place in Mississippi—the state symbolizing the blatant abuse of white power. . . . In that state more than forty Negroes and whites have either been lynched or murdered over the last three years, and not a single man has been punished for these crimes.

—*WDWG* II

Black Power is a nihilistic philosophy born out of the conviction that the Negro can't win . . . the view that American society is so hopelessly corrupt and enmeshed in evil that there is no possibility of salvation from within.

—*WDWG* II

. . . the only time I have been booed was one night in a Chicago mass meeting by some young members of the Black Power movement. I went home that night with an ugly feeling.

—*WDWG* II

For twelve years, I, and others like me, had held out radiant promises of progress. I had preached to them about my dream. I had lectured to them about the not too distant day when they would have freedom. . . . Their hopes had soared. They were now booing because they felt that we were unable to deliver on our promises. . . . But revolution, though born of despair, cannot long be sustained by despair.

—*WDWG* II

Yet behind Black Power's legitimate and necessary concern for group unity and black identity lies the belief that there can be a separate black road to power and fulfillment. Few ideas are more unrealistic.

—WDWG II

Black Power alone is no more insurance against social injustice than white power.

—WDWG II

One unfortunate thing about Black Power is that it gives priority to race prejudice at a time when the impact of automation and other forces have made the economic question fundamental for blacks and whites alike. In this context a slogan "Power for Poor People" would be much more appropriate.

—WDWG II

In the final analysis the weakness of Black Power is its failure to see that the black man needs the white man and the white man needs the black man.

—WDWG II

Probably the most destructive feature of Black Power is its unconscious and often conscious call for retaliatory violence.

—WDWG II

It is dangerous to organize a movement around self-defense. The line of demarcation between defensive violence and aggressive violence is very thin.

—WDWG II

Now the plain, inexorable fact is that any attempt of the American Negro to overthrow his oppressor with violence will not

work. We do not need President Johnson to tell us this by re-
minding Negro rioteers that they are outnumbered ten to one.

—*WDWG* II

The problem with hatred and violence is that they intensify the
fears of the white majority, and leave them less ashamed of their
prejudices toward Negroes.

—*WDWG* II

The greatest paradox of the Black Power movement is that it
talks unceasingly about not imitating the values of white society,
but in advocating violence it is imitating the worst, the most
brutal and most uncivilized value of American life.

—*WDWG* II

While I strongly disagree with their separatist black supremacy
philosophy, I have nothing but admiration for what our Muslim
brothers have done to rehabilitate ex-convicts, dope addicts, and
men and women who, through despair and self-hatred, have
sunk to moral degeneracy.

—*WDWG* IV

RIOTS

The limitations of riots, moral questions aside, is that they cannot win and their participants know it. Hence, rioting is not revolutionary but reactionary because it invites defeat.

—TOC I

The fourth cause [of the 1967 riots] is the war in Vietnam. Negroes are conscripted in double measure for combat. They constitute more than 20 percent of the front-line troops in a war of unprecedented savagery although their proportion in the population is 10 percent.

—TOC I

In all the riots, taken together, the property damage reached colossal proportions (exceeding a billion dollars). Yet the physical injury inflicted by Negroes upon white people was inconsequential by comparison. The bruising edge of the weapon of violence in Negro hands was employed almost exclusively against property—not persons.

—TOC I

Let us say boldly, that if the total slum violations of law by the white man over the years were calculated and compared with the lawbreaking of a few days of riots, the hardened criminal would be the white man.

—TOC I

Fewer people have been killed in ten years of nonviolent demonstrations across the South than were killed in one night rioting
in Watts [1965].

—WDWG II

There is something painfully sad about a riot. One sees scream-
ing youngsters and angry adults fighting hopelessly and aimlessly
against impossible odds. Deep down within them you perceive a
desire for self-destruction, a suicidal longing.

—WDWG II

WAR

The fear of darkness led to the discovery of the secret of electricity. The fear of pain led to the marvellous advances of medical science. The fear of ignorance was one reason that man built great institutions of learning. The fear of war was one of the forces behind the birth of the United Nations.

—*STL* XII

There may have been a time when war served as a negative good by preventing the spread and growth of an evil force, but the destructive power of modern weapons eliminates even the possibility that war may serve as a negative good.

—*STL* IV

A world war—God forbid!—will leave only smouldering ashes as a mute testimony of a human race whose folly led inexorably to untimely death. Yet there are those who sincerely feel that disarmament is an evil and international negotiation is an abominable waste of time.

—*STL* IV

But alas! Science cannot now rescue us, for even the scientist is lost in the terrible midnight of our age. Indeed, science gave us the very instruments that threaten to bring universal suicide.

—*STL* VI

SHENG--PALMISANO, NATHAN

Unclaim : 2/1/2020

Held date : 1/25/2020
Pickup location : Cedar Mill Library

Title : The Martin Luther King, Jr., c
ompanion : quotations from the speeches, essays,
and books of Martin Luther King, Jr.
Call number : 803.5 KING
Item barcode : 33614013326573
Assigned branch : Cedar Mill Library

Notes:

Our scientific power has outrun our spiritual power. We have
guided missiles and misguided man.

—STL VII

We say that war is a consequence of hate, but close scrutiny
reveals this sequence: First fear, then hate, then war, and finally
deeper hatred.

—STL XII

In this day of man's highest technical achievement, in this
day of dazzling discovery, of novel opportunities, loftier digni-
ties and fuller freedom for all, there is no excuse for the kind
of blind craving for power and resources that provoked the
wars of previous generations. There is no need to fight for
food and land.

—WDWG VI

The fact that most of the time human beings put the truth about
the nature and risks of the nuclear war out of their minds because
it is too painful and therefore not "acceptable" does not alter
the nature and risks of such war. The device of "rejection" may
temporarily cover up anxiety, but it does not bestow peace of
mind and emotional security.

—NL

A nation that continues year after year to spend more money on
military defense than on programs of social uplift is approaching
spiritual death.

—WDWG VI

Wisdom born of experience should tell us that war is obsolete.

—TOC V

Man is a child of God, made in His image, and therefore he must be respected as such. Until men see this everywhere, until nations see this everywhere, we will be fighting wars.

—*TOC* V

Equality will hardly solve the problem of either whites or Negroes if it is equality in a society under the spell of terror and a world doomed to extinction.

—NL

I still have a dream today that one day war will come to an end, that men will beat their swords into plowshares and their spears into pruning hooks, that nations will no longer rise up against nations, neither will they study war any more.

—*TOC* V

VIETNAM

. . . they wonder what kind of nation it is that applauds nonviolence whenever Negroes face white people in the streets of the United States, but then applauds violence and burning and death when these same Negroes are sent to the field of Vietnam.

—*WDWG* II

When I see our country today intervening in what is basically a civil war, mutilating hundreds of thousands of Vietnam children with napalm, burning villages and rice fields at random, painting the valleys of that small Asian country red with human blood, leaving broken bodies in countless ditches . . . and all this in the name of pursuing the goal of peace—I tremble for our world.

—*WDWG* VI

We were taking the black young men who had been crippled by our society and sending them eight thousand miles away to guarantee liberties in Southeast Asia which they had not found in southwest Georgia and East Harlem.

—*TOC* II

If we continue, there will be no doubt in my mind and in the mind of the world that we have no honorable intentions in Vietnam. It will become clear that our minimal expectation is to occupy it as an American colony.

—TOC II

The generation of the past twenty-five years cannot be understood unless we remember that it has lived during that period through the effects of four wars: World War II, the "cold" war, the Korean War, and Vietnam. No other generation of young Americans was ever exposed to a remotely similar traumatic experience.

—TOC III

We have destroyed their lands and their crops. We have cooperated in the crushing of the nation's only non-Communist revolutionary political force—the unified Buddhist Church. . . . We have corrupted their women and children and killed their men. What liberators!

—VL

Perhaps only his [Ho Chi Minh's] sense of humor and irony can save him when he hears the most powerful nation in the world speaking of *his* aggression as it drops thousands of bombs on a poor weak nation more than eight thousand miles away from its shores.

—VL

It's one of the strangest things that all the great military geniuses of the world have talked about peace. The conquerors of old who came killing in pursuit of peace, Alexander, Julius Caesar, Charlemagne, and Napoleon, were akin in seeking a peaceful world order. . . . Every time we drop bombs in Vietnam President Johnson talks eloquently about peace . . . but one day we must come to see that peace is not merely a distant goal we seek, but that it is a means by which we arrive at that goal. We must pursue peaceful ends through peaceful means.

—*TOC* V

If America's soul becomes totally poisoned, part of the autopsy must read Vietnam. It can never be saved so long as it destroys the hopes of men the world over.

—VL

PART SIX
REFLECTIONS

INTERNATIONAL COOPERATION

We are everlasting debtors to known and unknown men and women. . . . When we arise in the morning, we go into the bathroom where we reach for a sponge provided for us by a Pacific Islander. We reach for soap that is created for us by a Frenchman. The towel is provided by a Turk. Then at the table we drink coffee which is provided for us by a South American, or tea by a Chinese, or cocoa by a West African. Before we leave for our jobs, we are beholden to more than half the world.

—*STL* VII

More recently I have come to see the need for the method of nonviolence in international relations. . . . I am no doctrinaire pacifist, but I have tried to embrace a realistic pacifism which finds the pacifist position as the lesser evil in the circumstances.

—*STL* XV

We have waited for more than 340 years for our constitutional and God-given rights. The nations of Asia and Africa are moving with a jetlike speed toward gaining political independence, but we still creep at horse-and-buggy pace toward gaining a cup of coffee at a lunch counter.

—*WCW* V
"Letter from Birmingham Jail"

In measuring the full implications of the civil-rights revolution, the greatest contribution may be in the area of world peace. . . . Nonviolence, the answer to the Negro's need, may become the answer to the most desperate need of all humanity.

—*WCW* VIII

Sooner or later all the peoples of the world, without regard to the political systems under which they live, will have to discover a way to live together in peace. Man . . . has now reached the day when violence toward another human being must become as abhorrent as eating another's flesh.

—*WCW* VIII

The hard cold facts today indicate that the hope of the people of color in the world may well rest on the American Negro and his ability to reform imperialism from within and thereby turn the technology and wealth of the West to the task of liberating the world from want.

—*WDWG* II

For several centuries the direction of history flowed from the nations and societies of Western Europe out into the rest of the world in "conquests" of various sorts. That period, the era of colonialism, is at an end. East is moving West. The earth is being redistributed.

—*WDWG* VI

Two-thirds of the peoples of the world go to bed hungry every night. They are undernourished, ill-clothed, and shabbily clad. Many of them have no houses or beds. . . . There is nothing new about poverty. What is new, however, is that we now have the resources to get rid of it.

—*WDWG* VI

The time has come for an all-out world war against poverty. The rich nations must use their vast resources of wealth to develop the underdeveloped, school the unschooled, and feed the unfed.

—*WDWG* VI

Therefore I suggest that the philosophy and strategy of nonviolence become immediately a subject for study and for serious experimentation in every field of human conflict, by no means excluding the relations between nations.

—*WDWG* VI

We still have a choice today: nonviolent coexistence or violent coannihilation. This may well be mankind's last chance to choose between chaos and community.

—*WDWG* VI

We may now be in only the initial period of an era of change as far-reaching in its consequences as the American Revolution. The developed industrial nations of the world cannot remain secure islands of prosperity in a seething sea of poverty.

—*TOC* I

Granted that the easygoing optimism of yesterday is impossible. . . . Granted that we face a world crisis which leaves us standing so often amid the surging murmur of life's restless sea. But every crisis has both its dangers and its opportunities. It can spell either salvation or doom. In a dark confused world the kingdom of God may yet reign in the hearts of men.

—NL

I cannot forget that the Nobel Prize for Peace was also a commission—a commission to work harder than I had ever worked be-

fore for "the brotherhood of man." This is a calling which takes
me beyond national allegiances.

—*TOC* II

We in the West must bear in mind that the poor countries are
poor primarily because we have exploited them through political
or economic colonialism. Americans in particular must help
their nation repent of her modern economic imperialism.

—*TOC* IV

Can a nonviolent, direct-action movement find application on
the international level, to confront economic and political problems? I believe it can.

—*TOC* IV

Now let me suggest first that if we are to have peace on earth,
our loyalties must become ecumenical rather than sectional. Our
loyalties must transcend our race, our tribe, our class, and our
nation; and this means we must develop a world perspective.

—*TOC* V

More than a million people sleep on the sidewalks of Bombay
every night; more than half a million sleep on the sidewalks of
Calcutta every night. They have no houses to go into. They
have no beds to sleep in. As I beheld these conditions, something within me cried out: "Can we in America stand idly by
and not be concerned?" And an answer came: "Oh, no!"

—*TOC* V

It really boils down to this: that all life is interrelated. We are
all caught in an inescapable network of mutuality, tied into a
single garment of destiny. Whatever affects one directly, affects
all indirectly.

—*TOC* V

It is a sad fact that because of comfort, complacency, a morbid fear of communism, and our proneness to adjust to injustice, the Western nations that initiated so much of the revolutionary spirit of the modern world have now become the arch-antirevolutionaries.

—*TOC* II

My mother, as the daughter of a successful minister, had grown up in comparative comfort. She . . . had, in general, been protected from the worst blights of discrimination. But my father, a sharecropper's son, had met its brutalities firsthand, and had begun to strike back at an early age.

—STF I

I remember riding with him another day when he accidentally drove past a stop sign. A policeman pulled up to the car and said: "All right, boy, pull over and let me see your license." My father replied indignantly, "I'm no boy." Then, pointing to me, "This is a boy. I'm a man, and until you call me one, I will not listen to you." The policeman was so shocked that he wrote the ticket up nervously, and left the scene as quickly as possible.

—STF I

As a teenager I had never been able to accept the fact of having to go to the back of a bus or sit in the segregated section of a train. The first time I had been seated behind a curtain in a dining car, I felt as if the curtain had been dropped on my selfhood.

—STF I

The first twenty-four years of my life were years packed with fulfillment. I had no basic problems or burdens. . . . It was not until I became a part of the leadership of the Montgomery bus protest that I was actually confronted with the trials of life.

—*STL* XI

Most of all I am indebted to my wife, Coretta, without whose love, sacrifices, and loyalty neither life nor work would bring fulfillment. She has given me words of consolation when I needed them most, and a well-ordered home where Christian love is a reality.

—*STF,* Preface

Many times Coretta saw her good meals grow dry in the oven when a sudden emergency kept me away. Yet she never complained and she was always there when I needed her.

—*STF* VII
December 1955

The threats continued. Almost every day someone warned me that he had overheard white men making plans to get rid of me. Almost every night I went to bed faced with the uncertainty of the next moment. In the morning I would look at Coretta and "Yoki" and say to myself: "They can be taken from me at any moment; I can be taken away from them at any moment." For once, I did not even share my thoughts with Coretta.

—*STF* VIII
Early 1956

Ordinarily, a person leaving a courtroom with a conviction behind him would wear a somber face. But I left with a smile. I knew that I was a convicted criminal, but I was proud of my crime.

—*STF* VIII
March 22, 1956

As we neared the downtown area, Bull Connor ordered his men to arrest us. Ralph [Abernathy] and I were hauled off by two muscular policemen, clutching the backs of our shirts in handfuls. All the others were promptly arrested. . . . For more than twenty-four hours I was held incommunicado, in solitary confinement. . . . I suffered no physical brutality at the hands of my jailers. Some of the prison personnel were surly and abusive, but that was to be expected in southern prisons.

—WCW IV
Early May 1963

Due to my involvement in the struggle for the freedom of my people, I have known very few quiet days in the last few years. I have been imprisoned in Alabama and Georgia jails twelve times. My home has been bombed twice. A day seldom passes that my family and I are not the recipients of threats of death. I have been the victim of a near-fatal stabbing. So in a real sense I have been battered by the storms of persecution.

—STL XV

If only to save myself from bitterness, I have attempted to see my personal ordeals as an opportunity to transfigure myself and heal the people involved in the tragic situation which now obtains. I have lived these past few years with the conviction that unearned suffering is redemptive.

—STL XV

I don't know what will happen now. We've got some difficult days ahead. But it really doesn't matter with me now, because I've been to the mountaintop. And I don't mind. Like anybody, I would like to live a long life; longevity has its place. But I'm not concerned about that now. I just want to do God's will. And He's allowed me to go up to the mountain. And I've looked over. And I've seen the promised land. I may not get there with you. But I want you to know tonight that we as a people will get to the promised land. And I'm happy tonight. I'm not worried about anything, I'm not fearing any man. Mine eyes have seen the glory of the coming of the Lord!

—"I've Been to the Mountaintop"
The eve of his assassination
Memphis, Tennessee
April 3, 1968

THE FUTURE

Our freedom was not won a century ago, it is not won today; but some small part of it is in our hands, and we are marching no longer by ones and twos but in legions of thousands, convinced now it cannot be denied by any human force. Today the question is not whether we shall be free but by what course we will win.

—TOC I

America must seek its own ways of atoning for the injustices she has inflicted upon her Negro citizens. I do not suggest atonement for atonement's sake or because there is need for self-punishment. I suggest atonement as the moral and practical way to bring the Negro's standard up to a realistic level.

—WCW VIII

It is impossible to create a formula for the future which does not take into account that our society has been doing something special *against* the Negro for hundreds of years. How then can he be absorbed into the mainstream of American life if we do not do something special *for* him now? . . .

—WCW VIII

The sooner our society admits that the Negro Revolution is no momentary outburst soon to subside into placid passivity, the easier the future will be for us all.

—WCW VIII

History has thrust upon our generation an indescribably important destiny—to complete a process of democratization which our nation has too long developed too slowly. . . . How we deal with this crucial situation will determine our moral health as individuals, our cultural health as a region, our political health as a nation, and our prestige as a leader of the free world.

—*STF* XI

If you lose hope, somehow you lose the vitality that keeps life moving, you lose that courage to be, that quality that helps you to go on in spite of all. And so today I still have a dream.

—*TOC* V

. . . I say to you, my friends, so even though we face the difficulties of today and tomorrow, I still have a dream. It is a dream deeply rooted in the American dream.

I have a dream that one day this nation will rise up and live out the true meaning of its creed: "We hold these truths to be self-evident; that all men are created equal."

I have a dream that one day, on the red hills of Georgia, sons of former slaves and the sons of former slave-owners will be able to sit together at the table of brotherhood.

I have a dream that one day even the state of Mississippi, a state sweltering with the heat of injustice, sweltering with the heat of oppression, will be transformed into an oasis of freedom and justice.

I have a dream that my four little children will one day live in a nation where they will not be judged by the color of their skin but by the content of their character.

I have a dream today.

I have a dream that one day, down in Alabama, with its vicious racists, with its governor having his lips dripping with the words of interposition and nullification, one day right here in

Alabama, little black boys and black girls will be able to join hands with little white boys and white girls and walk together as sisters and brothers.

I have a dream today.

I have a dream that one day "every valley shall be exalted, every hill and mountain shall be made low, the rough places will be made plains, and the crooked places will be made straight, and the glory of the Lord shall be revealed, and all flesh shall see it together."

This is our hope. This is the faith that I go back to the South with. With this faith we will be able to hew out of the mountain of despair a stone of hope. With this faith we will be able to transform the jangling discords of our nation into a beautiful symphony of brotherhood. With this faith, we will be able to work together, to struggle together, to stand up for freedom together, knowing that we will be free one day.

And this will be the day. This will be the day when all of God's children will be able to sing with new meaning "My country 'tis of thee, sweet land of liberty, of thee I sing. Land where my fathers died, land of the pilgrim's pride, from every mountainside, let freedom ring."

And if America is to be a great nation this must become true. So let freedom ring from the prodigious hilltops of New Hampshire. Let freedom ring from the mighty mountains of New York. Let freedom ring from the heightening Alleghenies of Pennsylvania!

Let freedom ring from the snowcapped Rockies of Colorado!

Let freedom ring from the curvaceous slopes of California!

But not only that; let freedom ring from the Stone Mountain of Georgia! Let freedom ring from Lookout Mountain of Tennessee.

Let freedom ring from every hill and molehill of Mississippi. From every mountainside, let freedom ring. And when this happens, and when we allow freedom to ring, and when we let it ring from every village and every hamlet, from every state and every city, we will be able to speed up that day when all of God's children, black men and white men, Jews and Gentiles, Protestants and Catholics, will be able to join hands and sing in the words of that old Negro spiritual, "Free at last! Free at last! Thank God Almighty, we are free at last!"

—"I Have a Dream"
March on Washington
August 28, 1963

CHRONOLOGY

1929

15 January   Martin Luther King, Jr., born in Atlanta, Georgia.

1947

MLK works as assistant to his father, Rev. Martin Luther King, Sr., at the Ebenezer Baptist Church, Atlanta.

1948

June   MLK graduates from Morehouse College, Atlanta.

1951

June   MLK graduates from Crozer Theological Seminary, Chester, Pennsylvania.

1953

He marries Coretta Scott.

1954

May   In a landmark decision, the U.S. Supreme Court rules that racial segregation is unconstitutional in public schools (*Brown* v. *Board of Education*).

October   MLK becomes a pastor at the Dexter Avenue Church in Montgomery, Alabama.

1955

1 December   In Montgomery, Mrs. Rosa Parks is arrested because she refuses to give up her bus seat to a white man.

5 December   The bus boycott begins in Montgomery. MLK is made president of the Montgomery Improvement Association.

1956

January   MLK is arrested for "speeding" in a 25-mile zone.

30 January   A bomb lands on MLK's porch in Montgomery.

4 June   A U.S. district court decides that the segregation on municipal buses is unconstitutional.

13 November   This decision is upheld by the U.S. Supreme Court.

21 December   End of segregation on the Montgomery city buses.

1957

January   On MLK's porch, an unexploded bomb is found.

February   MLK is made president of the newly founded Southern Christian Leaderships Conference (SCLC).

June   MLK meets with Vice President Richard M. Nixon.

September   In order to escort nine black students to a white high school in Little Rock, Arkansas, President Eisenhower federalizes the Arkansas National Guard.

1958

23 June   MLK and other civil rights leaders confer with President Eisenhower.

20 September   MLK suffers chest wounds from a stabbing by a deranged woman in Harlem, New York.

1959

February–March   MLK and Coretta King study Mahatma Gandhi's nonviolence policies in India.

1960

January   MLK is made copastor to his father at the Ebenezer Baptist Church and moves his family to Atlanta.

May   An all-white jury acquits MLK of tax-evasion charges.

24 June   MLK confers with presidential candidate John F. Kennedy.

19 October   MLK is again arrested in Atlanta. Eight days later, he is released from State Prison on a $2 thousand bond.

1961

May   First freedom riders leave Washington, and are met with mob violence in Alabama.

16 December   MLK is arrested at a demonstration at Albany, Georgia.

1962

July   At an Albany prayer vigil, MLK is again arrested.

September   James Meredith tries to enroll at the University of Mississippi.

16 October   MLK confers with President Kennedy.

1963

March–April   MLK is arrested during demonstrations in Birmingham, Alabama. He writes his "Letter from Birmingham Jail" while in prison.

June   George C. Wallace, Governor of Alabama, attempts to interfere with the integration of the University of Alabama. President Kennedy federalizes the Alabama National Guard and Wallace withdraws.

28 August   The March on Washington. MLK's "I Have a Dream" speech.

22 November   President Kennedy assassinated.

1964

June   Three civil rights workers are missing in Philadelphia, Mississippi. Their bodies are found in August.

September   At the invitation of Berlin mayor Willy Brandt, MLK and his close friend Ralph Abernathy visit West Berlin.

18 September   MLK is received by Pope Paul VI.

10 December   MLK is awarded the Nobel Peace Prize.

1965

21 February   Black Muslim leader Malcolm X is murdered in New York.

March   On their march from Selma to Montgomery, Alabama, demonstrators are beaten up.

15 March   President Johnson announces the voting rights bill he is submitting to Congress.

21–25 March   Federal troops protect over three thousand demonstrators on their march from Selma to Montgomery.

6 August   President Johnson signs the Voting Rights Act.

11–16 August   Riots in Watts, the black district of Los Angeles, with thirty-five dead.

1966

16 May MLK's statement against the Vietnam war is read at a huge protest rally in Washington.

June The "Black Power" slogan is launched by Stokely Carmichael and others at Greenwood, Mississippi.

5 August Stones are thrown at MLK during a protest march in Chicago.

1967

25 March MLK attacks again President Johnson's Vietnam policy during a speech in Chicago.

10–11 May Riots at the all-black Jackson State College in Jackson, Mississippi.

12–17 July Riots in Newark, New Jersey, leaving twenty-three dead, and over seven hundred injured.

23–30 July Widespread riots in Detroit, leaving forty-three dead.

26 July MLK and other black leaders call for an end of the riots.

30 October The U.S. Supreme Court confirms the convictions of MLK and other civil rights leaders on contempt-of-court charges connected with the Birmingham demonstration of 1963. All convicted spend four days in jail.

1968

28 March In Memphis, Tennessee, MLK leads a large number of protesters in support of striking sanitation workers. Disorder breaks out and fifty people are injured.

3 April MLK delivers his last speech, at the Masonic Temple in Memphis, Tennessee (the "Mountaintop" speech).

4 April MLK is killed by a sniper at the Lorraine Motel in Memphis. James Earl Ray is later convicted of his murder.

1983

2 November By Act of Congress, the third Monday in January is made a legal holiday, as the birthday of Martin Luther King, Jr.

PHOTO CREDITS